Life

Thru

Poetry

A journey through one's
life in the eyes of a poet.

Talented, Tough, Tenacious, Tolerant
Home to few, envied by many.
She loves her family and provides for any.
A fearless mother, undefined like no other
A true gem, A miracle
Writer, Warrior, Wise, Whimsical
A beautiful being of the earth, lover of self-worth.
There is nothing she can't do and nothing she won't
prove, for her, the little girl she gave birth too.

She is the daughter of a peach, Georgia Mae.
Carrying the Lineage with her everyday
Spiritual, Strong, Solid, Supreme
A wombman of your wildest dreams
The highest of high often unglorified
Underrated, understanding, underestimated,
undefined, one who can turn back the hands of
time.

She is a researcher, a poet, a dreamer my mother.
She is a caretaker, a student, the power of thunder.
She is a role model, a leader, a pillar, a believer. She
is absolutely, breathtaking, forever a healer. She
is not only a fine specimen, but a phenomenal
woman,
For she is my mother the one and only.

Written and composed by Rae'chel M. Hoover

A Fan

Come take a walk with me, hold my hand. Tell me; are you my best friend or a fan.

A fan of how I carry myself and the way I walk. Looking at me longing, not finding the words to talk.

Take a walk with me, tell me your lifelong plan, are you going to make me the best part of your life or continue to be a fan.

Are you wasting my time calling me on the phone; telling me things like, you don't enjoy being alone?

Keeping me intrigued, by all the things you say, smiling and blushing throughout my day.
Am I a part of your lifelong plans; or will you continue to be just a Fan?

TH

A Kind Word

Hey beautiful, how was your day?

Did your boss like your work? Did he have good things to say?

What can I do to make you smile? Cook you dinner, sit and talk for a while.

Just relax, I will clean the dishes; I want you to have a wonderful evening as I try to fulfill your wishes.

TH

Backstabber's

All up in my face, smiling and conniving, running around lying while people are dying.

Chatting over here, Chatting over there, running your lips so much you need a spare.

Spending all your time digging up scars; why don't you stop looking so low and raise the bar.

Focus on your life and build your dreams, instead of being a backstabber u true nightmare to be seen.

TH

Beauty

You hate me because of my beauty, been your mom and fulfill my duties, I did not create myself; but for those who did I am blessed.

Appreciate me, don't hate to the point of evil is your fate; Spending your time to punish and all, creating negative vibes in the mind of anyone that heed your call.

You should be proud of the beauty on your mother; try being a friend and not just another: Another person out here in the streets, that she has to overcome in order to have peace.

TH

Behind closed doors.

Going out in public, everyone looks so nice. The children are so well spoken, and I am proud to say you are my wife,

The house is beautiful, so organized and clean; the lawn is well manicured, plants are lush and green.

Neighbors say we see you working so hard, how do you do it all: being a superstar. Little do they know I am living in hell, he's on drugs there is no one I can tell.

I try to keep a smile as if everything is good, things are disappearing, and we have no food.

The landlord came by to ask me about the rent, with everything else my money is spent. Give me some more time I will do what I can, I know my problems are not your plans.

Everything is not always what it seems Because behind closed doors, life is truly mean.   TH

By Myself

I feel all by myself, I have raised two
kids plus someone else.

I have been there for everybody and
everything, I do not know who I am and
all that I have seen.

Most of your years they use them all up,
and if you are not looking, it will be your
favorite cup.

Never having time: No time for you,
broken promises, and tons of excuse;
Really, they could care less about, how it
looks.

Hard and cold like a math book.

TH

Can you watch your children?

Mom ask, Can you watch the children? I have to go to work.

For eight hours, that's too long; Why don't you ask your momma: call her on the phone.

Can you watch the children while I take a nap? A nap noooo, you don't have time for that.

Wait until you go to bed, those kids play too much. the noise gets inside my head.

Can you watch the children I want to go back to school; Why you are asking me that now, for the last ten years you been a fool.

Woman do not ask me nothing about watching these kids, you're their mother, you know how it is.

TH

Darkness

My old friend: there you are waiting again.

Waiting for me to come out my door, just to see what you have in store.

Altering the thoughts in my mind, letting me know you are very unkind.

Keeping me wondering, always on edge, opening these doors I do Dred.

Darkness, Darkness my old friend, this is where you stop, and my life begins.

TH

Dating

When we were dating, everything was
good; Long days at work its understood.

Happy to see you, glad you are here, my
feelings for you are really sincere.

How are you doing? how's it going?   I am
just great seeing that I am your one and
only.

Putting in time, things are not the
same: we were dating, then it all changed.

What happened when everything was
good. That's when we were dating, and you
understood.

TH

Defeated

Every way I turn, I feel defeated.

People trying to steal my sanity, totally and completely.

I turn out the lights and sit alone, trying to recap where I went wrong.

It's so hard going from day to day, feeling totally defeated; I must pray.

Defeated and Deflated is how I feel, this must end for my true spirit to be revealed.

TH

Georgia

Always On My Mind.

Your soft skin and beautiful smile;
please **Mrs. Georgia** stay for a while.

You are always there to hold my hand,
see me through hard times and back
again.

Often taking me on a peaceful ride,
knowing my concerns and hearing my
cries.

Georgia, Always on my mind. How I
wish you were here; you are one of a
kind.

TH

Grateful

I am grateful: Grateful for my little girl, she really tries to do what is right, In this world. Often torn by her emotions and a face; Not sure if truth is even in this place.

Thoughtful and giving with a kind heart; people see her coming and go above and beyond to do their part.

Their part to deceive and not appreciate, her pleasing personality and her gentle state.

Her gorgeous smile and beautiful skin, and for that she is punished from the outside in.

Grateful for this little girl, embrace your angels and not the demons of this world.

TH

How Dare You?

Question me! What were you doing? How could this be? I know what you are saying, and I heard this story: but I need to do my own inventory.

Did you do 100 percent? Act like a woman and pay your portion of the rent?

Let me say this!!!! Not only did I do my job: but I carried you this far.

I wash, cook, and clean; worked two jobs and a part-time in between.

I was your support system, mother of your child, taking care of my business, while you were living foul.

Stealing, Lying and Pretending; showing a different face the false messages you were sending.

So, when you ask about my part. I carried a full deck, while you held one card.

TH

How I Feel

I often think about, How I Feel. When we first met, I knew it was real.

We would talk for hours lingering on the phone, not wanting to hang up and leave each other alone.

Taking walks, holding hands, I could not even think about another man.

Buying me flowers and tasty treats, you knew what to do, no one else could compete.

I often think about, How I feel, what I once had wasn't real.

TH

I Feel Good Today.

Even though nothing is going my way, I feel good today!

My clothes aren't name brand, the colors are faded and bland.

Money is nowhere to be found; I catch myself looking all around.

Getting a job, it isn't easy but being idle doesn't please me.

I feel good today and that's a start, I feel good today as I continue to do my part.

TH

I Love Me Some Me

I Love me some me, I am truly what others inspire to be.

Beautiful, witty, considerate, and strong, how can one possibly go wrong.

Charming, poised, determined and free, yes you to would like to be me.

Loyal, loving a true visionary you see, a mentor, mother, a believer in philosophy.

Always looking for that silver lining; not thinking about a thing called bad timing.

Just moving obstacles out my way, Pushing forward day to day.

Blessing you with my warm smile; How was your day, mine was worthwhile.

I Just Love me some me; always forever most definitely.

TH

I Raised Mine.

I raised mine and didn't want anymore,
because it was hard being single and poor.

Working two jobs, going to school; Instead of
hanging out and acting cool.

I shouldn't have to share my check with you
and yours; just because you were feeling him
on all fours.

I listened when my mom said don't bring no
kids in my house; you should have listened
instead of running your mouth.

So, before you ask one more time, get yours I
raised mine.

TH

I thought I knew

I thought I knew you and all your flaws.

I thought I knew you, because we shared the same space; sat across from you at dinner, watch you clean your plate.

I thought I knew you; from all the stories you shared, how everyone treated you badly and no one cares.

I thought I knew you; I don't know you at all, you have deep dark issues and many extra flaws.

TH

I Was Happy

I was happy as a young girl, I loved life and all the wonderful things in this world.

I loved people and having fun; working, dating, and shopping kept me on the run.

My heart was big and full of joy; just helpful, hopeful, happy, life was my toy.

I was cute, stylish, smart and clever, just a beautiful young lady a true treasure.

I was Happy as a young girl; I was once happy in this world.

TH

Insane

I close the shades and lock the doors, can't even stand people walking gently across the floor.

Coming home early, running from the dark: watching every car that pulls up and park. Looking at every man and thinking the same, he is a liar and truly insane.

Taking each day and playing the game, just trying to make it and endure the pain.

Living my life according to someone else's agenda only to realize they want you to surrender.

TH

It's A Struggle

It's A struggle every day, to get up and start my day with a smile.

I want to be bitter and just lay here for a while.

It's so easy to wallow here in my anger and think woe is me, it's more deserving to pick myself up and be free.

TH

Just Me

Sometimes I speak harsh, but I tell the truth!!!!!!!

Sometimes I love too hard because that's what I do.

I have high expectations, most certainly: I think highly of you and love me.

I stand on loyalty, morals, and dignity: without it who would I be!!!! Someone pretentious and fake, being a part of something I wish not to partake........

No that's not me, not at all. I am Just Me, sign my name write it on a wall.

So be yourself and stand tall!! Stand for nothing and try not to fall.

TH

Last to Shine.

From the man to the Kids, you are always behind.

Everyone takes you for granted, you are last in line.

I have done my job I just want to be.

Here comes someone else, can you do this for me.

What do want, wasting all my time: Taking me for granted.

Leaving me the last to shine.

TH

Look At My Place

My husband did that, Oh yes, he did;
this one is bigger than the last one; It's
just too good.

High ceilings, nice floors and walls,
rooms galore oh who do I call. I am
blessed Look at my place, we worked
so hard, to be in this space.

Working two jobs, not spending time,
this is great, it's blowing my mind.

Look at my place, look at it all, I am just
thankful. All in All

TH

MoM

Hey Mom
I need some money can you help me out, sure
without a doubt?
I need to use your car please; you can use it, just
do not bring it back on E.
I need you to watch my kids: for how long? okay
bring them over, I'll be at home.
I need a place to stay I am going through some
things: okay come on, it's all growing pains.

Hey Daughter
I don't feel good, I should go to the doctor. Yes,
you should and call me after.
Hey, my child can you come help me around the
house; What momma: I don't have time I am
trying to be with my spouse.
I was thinking we could go on a vacation
together; really let me call Ron Ron, Tisha and
Mayweather.

TH

Mother

My mother, the love of my life.

She taught me everything in
my childhood and on to being a wife.

A strong woman: with a heart of gold, a
pillar in the community, never one to
fold.

She lived her life with meaning and a
purpose; a blessing, teacher, mentor just
to scratch the surface.

A leader, a pioneer, a friend of mine. My
dear mother a love of all times.

TH

Mother's Day

It is just another day for me.

I have children that I really do not see; you would think I was the worst mother of the century.

If it were not for my husband bringing me flowers, it would be just another day fill with rain showers.

No big dinner or family plans, just another day is where it stands; I should be elated if my phone rings with someone saying Happy Mother's Day, or shall I sing.

It is so common for it to be just another day, I guess I am blessed to see it come into play.

TH

Best Friend

Hello my old friend.

Last time I saw you we were in college;
Me with my big smile and you with all the
knowledge.

Time has passed and we have grown, now
mothers and taking care of our home.

I remember all the times we shared; both
of us young living life without a care.

During the times we have been apart, you
were always my friend, with a special
place in my heart.

So, I hope you know on this day, you are
my true friend and friends we will stay.

TH

My Little Girl

I know she is damaged, devastated and confused. She would never think, her own father would abuse.

Abuse her mother right in front of her eyes, battered and bloody for drugs and supplies.

Her life would never be the same, the man she called father is in jail and her mother is in pain.

Answers and resolution, she try to find, with terrible thoughts running through her mind.

Stuck and shattered; still a little girl, often wondering is their true love in this world.

TH

My *Valentine*

Hello world, it is such a beautiful Day.

All dressed up in red, with nice things to say.

Buying cards and a bouquet of flowers to express our love and emotional power.

Making it official, standing in front of a courthouse judge.

I Love You; No, I Love You, It's A beautiful Day filled with Love.

TH

She left today

She left today and I am not sure why,
her heart took wings and decided to fly.

The kindest spirit, the warmest smile,
always loving, one of god's child.

She is my sister, my buddy, my friend;
someone I loved from birth till the end.

I will miss her, each and every day, a true
angel has flown away.

TH

Son

My grandson was just a baby and now a young
man. He has experienced a lot, not sure if
that was part of his life plan.

He came into his life innocent as can be, smiling
laughing just a happy baby.

Trusting that people will love and teach him the
things he needs to know, be there for him while
he makes mistakes and grow.

Sit and talk all about his day, take in a movie or
go to the park and play.

He has learned a lot in his short years,
overcoming obstacles and facing his fears.

You cannot trust a person to always be there but
believe in yourself and always stay aware.

TH

Stepdad.

Because I love your mother, I love you to, this is what I am willing to do.

Buy a house and call it home, so you and your friends would have a place to roam.

Work hard and pay the bills, to teach you the values of life and what's real.

Support your ideas and your thoughts, looking over the shortcomings and displacing the faults.

Providing you with your basic needs all the while keeping you at ease.

Taking you on trips and spending time, this newfound family is a true find.

Loving you like you were my very own, I am here for you anytime you call home.

TH

Sunshine

Feeling the sun on my face, Oh my what a beautiful space?

This space I am in has developed over time, it's so sunny and warm. It's a true friend of mine.

I have looked for you, for so long. Cried out for your rays to make me strong.

Shine on me and take away the dark, sunshine, restore my faith and warm my heart.

TH

Vows

You said I do, through thick and thin.

You never said you were going to be my beginning and my end.

You said I will love you through good times and bad.

You never said one day I will make you sad.

You said today I take you to be my wife.

You never said today, with my hands I will take your life.

TH

What Is This?

What Is this I feel; It's really cold,
there is so much, must be my soul.

Its pouring from my body and I can't
stop it, looks like blood flowing on
the carpet.

What is happening, how could this
be, all this blood is leaving me.

I don't recall what took place, for me
to be down here on my face.

If someone doesn't help me
soon: my body will be prepped and
in a tomb.

TH

What's My Name?

Who am I, what is my name, is it all one of
the same? I have all these labels on my back,
sometimes it's hard to stay on track.

Looking, searching for where I belong, in the
meantime hurting others and finding out
what is right and wrong.

Stripping myself of what completes
me: thinking my actions will let me be;
someone out on my own path and separating
me from the last.

Not knowing these ties run deep and long,
these labels is what made me strong. All this
made me who I am. I was raised by mother
and not the man.

So again, I ask what's my name, my
personality, my label its all the same.

TH

When We Met

I often think about, How I Feel. When
we first met, I knew it was real.

We would talk for hours lingering on
the phone, not wanting to hang up and
leave each other alone.

Taking walks, holding hands, I could not
even think about another man.

Buying me flowers and tasty treats, you
knew what to do, no one else could
compete.

I often think about, How I feel, what I
once had wasn't real.

TH

Where Are You?

Where are you on this journey?

Did you think for once, you would
need an attorney?

To rid yourself of this thing you once
loved. you swear it was a blessing
from the heavens above.

You wrote on paper; he is my one
and only. I wear his name I will
never be lonely.

You took this journey, only to find
you were misled and truly blind.

Blinded by the fluff and the thrills,
on a journey that had no true
appeal.

TH

Why is it so hard

Why is everything so hard: Oh, let me
see where do I start.

Working forty hours to pay the
rent, nothing left, not even a cent.
Picking and choosing another bill to
pay, barely making it day to day.

Clothes and shoes are a luxury, which
is something that will never
be.   Children, medical and dental; can
someone help me with this rental.

Heat, water, electric and air; why,
why, is this so unfair. I have to keep
moving and do my part but can
someone tell me; Why it has to be so
hard.

TH

You Never Been Good To Me

You never really been good to me; It was all conditionally.

Always what I can do for you and what you can take.

Never having time, even though I bought the plate.

Not sure where you came from and who you are,
but you never, been good to me
near or far.

TH

Your Creation

What did you create with all this abuse?
Three generations that feel they have no
use.

Going out into the world full of anger. not
thinking of the consequences embracing
danger.

Bickering, fighting, hurting one another,
wasting time, and moving further.

Further away trying to mask the pain, of
seeing your face and trying to restrain.

Restraining the emotions that comes with
it all; knowing your creation; created this
wall.

TH

In closing I want to thank all, that have purchased and read my work, and to those that have supported me on this journey.

Thanks to my parents, for blessing me with their witty personality, character, charm, and creativity. Also, the ability to experience life and live in a way they expect and that is pleasing to them.

Life Is Truly A Blessing if you live it Accordingly and treat everyone how you. Yourself would like to be treated.

I am who I am, with no apologies or compromise.

The Visit

It was all a plan; to see where you at and where you stand.

Seeing your growth was all worthwhile, looking at your face I cherish your smile.

Just to know you are okay, lifts my spirits and brightens my day.

It has been a pleasure to be in your space; sharing your creations the design of your place.

I am so proud of my little girl: that is now a woman and a blessing to this world.

TH